"Ye men of Galilee, why stand ye gazing up into heaven?
this same Jesus, which is taken up from you into heaven,
shall so come in like manner as ye have seen him
go into heaven." Acts 1:11

THIS SAME
JESUS

Gloria Copeland

KENNETH
COPELAND
PUBLICATIONS

Unless otherwise noted, all scripture is from the *King James Version* of the Bible.

Scripture quotations marked *The Amplified Bible* are from *The Amplified Bible, Old Testament* © 1965, 1987 by The Zondervan Corporation. *The Amplified New Testament* © 1958, 1987 by The Lockman Foundation. Used by permission.

This Same Jesus

ISBN-10 1-57562-243-2   30-0547
ISBN-13 978-1-57562-243-9

14 13 12 11 10 09   9 8 7 6 5 4

Kenneth Copeland Publications
Fort Worth, TX 76192-0001

For more information about Kenneth Copeland Ministries call 800-600-7395 or visit www.kcm.org.

This Same Jesus

by Gloria Copeland

One of the most wonderful things about Jesus is that He never changes. I love that about Him! He's not kind one day and harsh the next. He's not ready to heal one minute and reluctant the next. He's always "Jesus Christ [the Anointed One] the same yesterday, and today, and for ever" (Hebrews 13:8).

He is the same as He was in the Gospels of Matthew, Mark, Luke and John. There, we see a Jesus who is easily entreated. We see Him healing and delivering people at every turn. The people who came to Him on the dusty roads of Galilee didn't have to struggle and convince Him to help them. They simply asked and He answered. It was easy for them to receive from Jesus.

Jesus never said no to the people who came to Him in faith. He always supplied their need.

Religious tradition has taught us that at some point during the past 2,000 years, Jesus changed. That instead of healing people, He started telling them no when they asked for healing. He supposedly decided their sickness was teaching them something. Religious tradition has said the days of Jesus' miracles have passed away.

But that's just not true.

As I was reading the book of Acts one day, the Lord strongly reminded me of that. In fact, He used the first chapter to impress it on my heart in a fresh way. In those verses, we see Jesus preparing to leave the earth to go sit at the Father's right hand. He is speaking to the disciples, saying:

Ye shall receive power, after that the Holy Ghost is come upon you: and ye shall be witnesses unto me both in Jerusalem, and in all Judaea, and in Samaria, and unto the uttermost part of the earth. And when he had spoken these things, while they beheld, he was taken up; and a cloud received him out of their sight. And while they looked stedfastly toward heaven as he went up, behold, two men stood by them in white apparel; which also said, Ye men of Galilee, why stand ye gazing up into heaven? *this same Jesus, which is taken up from you into heaven, shall so come in like manner as ye have seen him go into heaven* (Acts 1:8-11).

Don't Reason It Away

Consider for a moment what the angel

said. I know you've probably heard it many times before, but I want you to let it sink in as a revelation in your heart. He said, "This same Jesus..." is going to come back. *This same Jesus!*

Let me ask you something. If Jesus was one way when He was on the earth, and He is going to be the same way when He comes back, what do you think He's going to be like during the time in between?

He's going to be the same!

This same Jesus! He's the same right now as He was when He walked the earth. He has the same heart of compassion. He's just as easily moved now as He was then. He's just as quick to heal now as He ever was. He truly is the same yesterday, and today, and forever.

That's such a simple revelation. We ought to just receive it like little children and believe it. But most of us don't. We start reasoning it away in our minds. We think, *Well, my disease is so serious and I've had it for such a long time, it just couldn't be that easy for me to be healed.*

Thoughts like that are lies of the devil! Jesus healed a number of people who had been sick for a long time. It wasn't hard for Him. Nothing was hard for Him. We need to quit reasoning so much and just believe!

"But Gloria," you may say, "how can Jesus minister to me the way He did to those who walked with Him 2,000 years ago? He isn't here anymore. He's in heaven."

Yes, He is in heaven, but He is still ministering here on the earth through His Word, and through the Holy Spirit who is working through the Church. That's why He could say to the disciples just before His ascension, "...lo, I am with you always, even unto the end of the world" (Matthew 28:20).

Read through the Gospels and then through Acts and you'll see that Jesus' ministry didn't change after He ascended to heaven. He just continued to do through the Church what

He had done personally during His earthly ministry. Through believers, He continued to heal, deliver and cast out devils by the power of the Holy Ghost.

Thank God that Holy Ghost power is still in our midst. Thank God the same anointing that was on Jesus is on the Church. This same Jesus is still available to minister to us and through us today!

He Went About Doing Good

With that in mind, we can take a fresh look at what Jesus said and did during His time on earth. Let's start with Luke 4, where we see the foundational message Jesus preached everywhere He went:

> The Spirit of the Lord [is] upon Me, because He has anointed Me [the Anointed One, the Messiah] to preach the good news (the Gospel)

to the poor; He has sent Me to announce release to the captives and recovery of sight to the blind, to send forth as delivered those who are oppressed [who are downtrodden, bruised, crushed, and broken down by calamity], to proclaim the accepted and acceptable year of the Lord [the day when salvation and the free favors of God profusely abound (verses 18-19, *The Amplified Bible*).

Now remember, Jesus is still preaching that message today. So if you fall into any of the categories He listed there—if you're blind, oppressed by sickness, depressed, in bondage to drugs or alcohol, or simply beaten down by the calamity of this world—Jesus is here to deliver you.

Today is the day of your salvation!

This is the day when the free favors

of God profusely abound. Those favors haven't stopped. They're still flowing today as freely as they were when Jesus first spoke those words.

If you want to see just how freely those divine favors flow, and how easy it is to obtain them, just read Matthew, Mark, Luke and John and watch Jesus in action. Acts 10:38 says of Him, "How God anointed Jesus of Nazareth with the Holy Ghost and with power: who went about doing good, and healing all that were oppressed of the devil; for God was with him."

Jesus just went about doing good. He would simply go from one place to another blessing people and healing them and delivering them. It wasn't hard to get Him to work miracles. It was easy!

Look at one day in Jesus' life, as recorded in Mark 1, and you can see for yourself:

On the sabbath day [Jesus] entered into the synagogue, and taught. And there was in their synagogue a man with an unclean spirit; and he cried out. And Jesus rebuked [the unclean spirit], saying, Hold thy peace, and come out of him. And when the unclean spirit had torn him, and cried with a loud voice, he came out of him. And they were all amazed, insomuch that they questioned among themselves, saying, What thing is this?...for with authority commandeth he even the unclean spirits, and they do obey him (verses 21, 23, 25-27).

Notice what Jesus did there. He came across a man who needed a burden removed and a devil cast out of him, so He simply did it. He didn't stop there, either. The Scripture tells us He went on that day "into the house of Simon...But Simon's wife's mother lay sick of a fever, and anon they tell him of her. And he came and took her by the hand, and lifted her up; and immediately the fever left her" (verses 29-31).

Isn't that something? The very next place He went, Jesus ran into another need. What did He do about it? He took care of it! He ministered healing. But His day wasn't over yet.

The next verses tell us that "At even, when the sun did set, they brought unto him all that were diseased, and them that were possessed with devils. And all the city was gathered together at the door. And he healed many that were sick of divers diseases, and cast out many devils" (verses 32-34).

With the eye of my heart, I love to see Jesus walking around, loving people and ministering to them. I love to see Him going about His day casting out devils, bringing healing and working miracles!

What's more, I love to think about the fact that Jesus still wants to spend His day that way. He's still the same Jesus!

What Do You Want
Him to Do for You?

It's just as easy to receive from Jesus today as it ever was. Back in the days when He walked the earth, Jesus would just be going from one place to another and people would rush up to Him with faith in their hearts, and in their mouths—and He'd do whatever they asked Him to do.

It was as simple as that! He did whatever they asked for in faith.

You can see that in the life of blind Bartimaeus. The Bible says he was sitting by the highway begging one day when Jesus came walking by: "And when he heard that it was Jesus of Nazareth, he began to cry out, and say, Jesus, thou son of David, have mercy on me. And many charged him that he should hold his peace: but he cried the more a great deal, Thou son of David, have mercy on me" (Mark 10:47-48).

Look what happened when Bartimaeus cried out: "And Jesus stood still, and commanded him to be called" (verse 49). That's always the way Jesus was. No matter what He was doing, when a person cried out in faith, Jesus would stop and minister to that person. He's still that way. At the call of faith today, all of heaven moves to answer that prayer.

When they brought Bartimaeus to Jesus, do you know what He said? Jesus asked him, "What wilt thou that I should do unto thee?" (verse 51). In *The Amplified Bible* it reads, "What do you want Me to do for you?" "The blind man said unto him, Lord, that I might receive my sight. And Jesus said unto him, Go thy way; thy faith hath made thee whole. And immediately he received his sight, and followed Jesus in the way" (verses 51-52).

Isn't that easy? Jesus asked Bartimaeus what he wanted. Bartimaeus answered...and Jesus did it.

Glory to God! Jesus has that same attitude toward us today. Every morning when you get up, He's saying, *What do you want Me to do for you?*

Now you can see how foolish it is for you to go to work without praying and telling Him what He can do for you today. If you just ignore Him and go on about your busy life, you won't receive anything from Him because He works by faith. You have to talk to Him like Bartimaeus did—and you have to believe He'll answer!

Jesus Is an Easy Touch

Someone might say, "Now wait a minute. The healing of Bartimaeus alone doesn't prove Jesus always responded like that. It's just one incident."

I know it, but if I had the time and space, I could give you many, many others. I could tell you about the leper in Matthew 8 who came to Jesus "and worshipped him, saying, Lord, if thou wilt, thou canst make me clean" (verse 2).

Do you know what Jesus' response was to him? "I will; be thou clean. And immediately his leprosy was cleansed" (verse 3).

I could tell you about the centurion who had a sick servant and came to Jesus, saying, "Lord...speak the word only, and my servant shall be healed" (verse 8).

Jesus didn't say to that man, "Now listen here—I'm the One who decides what needs to happen in these situations and I need to go lay My hands on that servant." No, He simply did what the centurion asked Him to do. He said, "Go thy way; and as thou hast believed, so be it done unto thee. And his servant was healed in the selfsame hour" (verse 13).

I could tell you about Jairus who fell at Jesus' feet "and besought him greatly, saying, My little daughter lieth at the point of death: I pray thee, come and lay thy hands on her, that she may be healed; and she shall live" (Mark 5:23). Even though that little girl died before Jesus arrived, He still did exactly what that man said. He took her by the hand, healed her and raised her from the dead!

I could tell you about the woman who had an issue of blood for 12 years and said to herself, "If I may touch but [Jesus'] clothes, I shall be whole" (verse 28). No doubt by now, even if you haven't read the story, you can guess what happened to the woman.

She was healed when she touched Jesus'

clothes, just like she said she'd be! "And he said unto her, Daughter, thy faith hath made thee whole; go in peace, and be whole of thy plague" (verse 34).

Do you see how easy Jesus was to deal with back then? He's just as easy to deal with now. He is easily touched with the feeling of our infirmities (Hebrews 4:15). Whatever those people said is what Jesus said and did. And whatever you say with your mouth and believe with your heart, He'll do for you. How do I know? Because He's the same Jesus.

Whatever you need from Him today— whether it's healing in your body, deliverance from oppression, devils, drugs, pornography, or anything else that has attached itself to your life—Jesus is saying, *What can I do for you? What is it that you want from Me?*

If you need money in your bank account, Jesus can handle it. He knows how to get money to you. If you'll give Him faith, and you'll give Him words to work with, He'll get you whatever you need.

If you need your children to come into the kingdom of God, Jesus knows how to rescue them. He knows how to bring in your children. He's saying, *What can I do for you today?*

Whatever you want, ask for it. Believe you receive it, and put it in your mouth! Start saying what you want Jesus to bring to pass.

This same Jesus! Jesus Christ, the Anointed One, the same yesterday, today and forever, desires to move in your life—to remove the burdens and destroy the yokes the devil has used to oppress you. He would like to see "the free favors of God profusely abound" in your life. He desires to bless you.

That was His ministry 2,000 years ago. It's still His ministry today. That's what He does every day, 24 hours a day.

Call on Him in faith and let Him do it for you. *He is the same, wonderful Jesus!*

Prayer for Salvation and Baptism in the Holy Spirit

Heavenly Father, I come to You in the Name of Jesus. Your Word says, "Whosoever shall call on the name of the Lord shall be saved" (Acts 2:21). I am calling on You. I pray and ask Jesus to come into my heart and be Lord over my life according to Romans 10:9-10: "If thou shalt confess with thy mouth the Lord Jesus, and shalt believe in thine heart that God hath raised him from the dead, thou shalt be saved. For with the heart man believeth unto righteousness; and with the mouth confession is made unto salvation." I do that now. I confess that Jesus is Lord, and I believe in my heart that God raised Him from the dead.

I am now reborn! I am a Christian—a child of Almighty God! I am saved! You also said in Your Word, "If ye then, being evil, know how to give good gifts unto your children: HOW MUCH MORE shall your heavenly Father give the Holy Spirit to them that ask him?" (Luke 11:13). I'm also asking You to fill me with the Holy Spirit. Holy Spirit, rise up within me as I praise God. I fully expect to speak with other tongues as You give me the utterance (Acts 2:4). In Jesus' Name. Amen!

Begin to praise God for filling you with the Holy Spirit. Speak those words and syllables you receive—not in your own language, but the language given to you by the Holy Spirit. You have to use your own voice. God will not force you to speak. Don't be concerned with how it sounds. It is a heavenly language!

Continue with the blessing God has given you and pray in the spirit every day.

You are a born-again, Spirit-filled believer. You'll never be the same!

Find a good church that boldly preaches God's Word and obeys it. Become part of a church family who will love and care for you as you love and care for them.

We need to be connected to each other. It increases our strength in God. It's God's plan for us.

Make it a habit to watch the *Believer's Voice of Victory* television broadcast and become a doer of the Word, who is blessed in his doing (James 1:22-25).

About the Author

Gloria Copeland is a noted author and minister of the gospel whose teaching ministry is known throughout the world. Believers worldwide know her through Believers' Conventions, Victory Campaigns, magazine articles, teaching audios and videos, and the daily and Sunday *Believer's Voice of Victory* television broadcast, which she hosts with her husband, Kenneth Copeland. She is known for "Healing School," which she began teaching and hosting in 1979 at KCM meetings. Gloria delivers the Word of God and the keys to victorious Christian living to millions of people every year.

Gloria is author of the New York Times best-seller, *God's Master Plan for Your Life*, as well as numerous favorites, including *God's Will for You, Walk With God, God's Will Is Prosperity, Hidden Treasures* and *To Know Him*. She has also co-authored several books with her husband, including *Family Promises, Healing Promises* and the best-selling daily devotionals, *From Faith to Faith* and *Pursuit of His Presence*.

She holds an honorary doctorate from Oral Roberts University. In 1994, Gloria was voted Christian Woman of the Year, an honor conferred on women whose example demonstrates outstanding Christian leadership. Gloria is also the co-founder and vice president of Kenneth Copeland Ministries in Fort Worth, Texas.

Learn more about Kenneth Copeland Ministries by visiting our Web site at **www.kcm.org**

Materials to Help You Receive Your Healing
by Gloria Copeland

Books

* And Jesus Healed Them All
  God's Prescription for Divine Health
  God's Will for Your Healing
* Harvest of Health
  Words That Heal (gift book with CD enclosed)

Audio Resources

Be Made Whole—Live Long, Live Healthy
God Is a Good God
God Wants You Well
Healing Confessions (CD and minibook)
Healing School

Video Resources

Be Made Whole—Live Long, Live Healthy
Know Him As Healer

DVD Resources

Be Made Whole—Live Long, Live Healthy
Know Him As Healer

Books Available From Kenneth Copeland Ministries

Kenneth Copeland

A Ceremony of Marriage
A Matter of Choice
Covenant of Blood
Faith and Patience—The Power Twins
Freedom From Fear
Giving and Receiving
Honor—Walking in Honesty, Truth and Integrity
How to Conquer Strife
How to Discipline Your Flesh
How to Receive Communion
In Love There Is No Fear
Know Your Enemy
Living at the End of Time—A Time of
    Supernatural Increase
Love Letters From Heaven
Love Never Fails
Mercy—The Divine Rescue of the Human Race
Now Are We in Christ Jesus
One Nation Under God (gift book with CD enclosed)
Our Covenant With God
Partnership—Sharing the Vision, Sharing the Grace
Prayer—Your Foundation for Success
Prosperity: The Choice Is Yours
Rumors of War
Sensitivity of Heart
Six Steps to Excellence in Ministry
Sorrow Not! Winning Over Grief and Sorrow
The Decision Is Yours

* Available in Spanish

by Gloria Copeland

ooks Co-Authored by Kenneth and Gloria Copeland

* Available in Spanish

He Did It All for You
One Word From God Can Change Your Life

One Word From God Series:
- One Word From God Can Change Your Destiny
- One Word From God Can Change Your Family
- One Word From God Can Change Your Finances
- One Word From God Can Change Your Formula
  for Success
- One Word From God Can Change Your Health
- One Word From God Can Change Your Nation
- One Word From God Can Change Your Prayer Life
- One Word From God Can Change
  Your Relationships

Load Up—A Youth Devotional
Over the Edge—A Youth Devotional
Pursuit of His Presence—A Daily Devotional
Pursuit of His Presence—A Perpetual Calendar
Raising Children Without Fear

Other Books Published by KCP

John G. Lake—His Life, His Sermons, His
    Boldness of Faith
The Holiest of All by Andrew Murray
The New Testament in Modern Speech
    by Richard Francis Weymouth
The Rabbi From Burbank by Isidor Zwirn and Bob Owen
Unchained! by Mac Gober

Products Designed for Today's Children and Youth

And Jesus Healed Them All (confession book and CD gift package)
Baby Praise Board Book
Baby Praise Christmas Board Book
Noah's Ark Coloring Book
The Best of *Shout!* Adventure Comics
The *Shout!* Giant Flip Coloring Book
The *Shout!* Joke Book
The *Shout!* Super-Activity Book
Wichita Slim's Campfire Stories

Commander Kellie and the Superkids_{SM} Books:

The SWORD Adventure Book
*Commander Kellie and the Superkids*_{SM}
   Solve-It-Yourself Mysteries
*Commander Kellie and the Superkids*_{SM} Adventure Series:
   Middle Grade Novels by Christopher P.N. Maselli:

#1 The Mysterious Presence
#2 The Quest for the Second Half
#3 Escape From Jungle Island
#4 In Pursuit of the Enemy
#5 Caged Rivalry
#6 Mystery of the Missing Junk
#7 Out of Breath
#8 The Year Mashela Stole Christmas
#9 False Identity
#10 The Runaway Mission
#11 The Knight-Time Rescue of Commander Kellie

World Offices
Kenneth Copeland Ministries

For more information about KCM and our products, please
write to the office nearest you:

Kenneth Copeland Ministries
Fort Worth, TX 76192-0001

Kenneth Copeland
Locked Bag 2600
Mansfield Delivery Centre
QUEENSLAND 4122
AUSTRALIA

Kenneth Copeland
Post Office Box 15
BATH
BA1 3XN
U.K.

Kenneth Copeland
Private Bag X 909
FONTAINEBLEAU
2032
REPUBLIC OF
SOUTH AFRICA

Kenneth Copeland
PO Box 3111 STN LCD 1
Langley BC V3A 4R3
CANADA

Kenneth Copeland Ministries
Post Office Box 84
L'VIV 79000
UKRAINE

We're Here for You!

Believer's Voice of Victory Television Broadcast

Join Kenneth and Gloria Copeland and the *Believer's Voice of Victory* broadcasts Monday through Friday and on Sunday each week, and learn how faith in God's Word can take your life from ordinary to extraordinary. This teaching from God's Word is designed to get you where you want to be—*on top!*

You can catch the *Believer's Voice of Victory* broadcast on your local, cable or satellite channels.* Also available 24 hours on webcast at BVOV.TV.

*Check your local listings for times and stations in your area.

Believer's Voice of Victory Magazine

Enjoy inspired teaching and encouragement from Kenneth and Gloria Copeland and guest ministers each month in the *Believer's Voice of Victory* magazine. Also included are real-life testimonies of God's miraculous power and divine intervention in the lives of people just like you!

It's more than just a magazine—it's a ministry.

To receive a FREE subscription to
Believer's Voice of Victory, write to:

Kenneth Copeland Ministries
Fort Worth, TX 76192-0001
Or call:
800-600-7395
(7 a.m.-5 p.m. CT)
Or visit our Web site at:
www.kcm.org

If you are writing from outside the U.S., please contact the KCM office nearest you. Addresses for all Kenneth Copeland Ministries offices are listed on the previous pages.